The Freelancer's Bible:

Making a Living as a Freelance Writer Online

Tiffani Velez

DEDICATION

For my children. Do whatever you dream of doing, because you're all brilliant and wonderful and so capable of all good things.

CONTENTS

CONTENTS

ACKNOWLEDGMENTS

Thank you so much to my designer, Gayle Hendricks. This book is beautiful, because you're a genius.
Thank you to my editor, Elaine Papciak. Your attention to typos and content is much appreciated.

Freelancers, I hope you find what you are looking for in this little book. Many blessings to you, wherever you are on your writing journey.
*All quotes were obtained at BrainyQuote.com

Chapter One

My Story

"When you do things from your soul, you feel a river moving in you."
Rumi

If you're like me, you're tempted to skip this part and go straight to the tips, but it's important to understand that I know where you're coming from. You'll find as many tips in this introduction as you will in the subsequent chapters, so stick with me, and you'll be all the more informed about the freelancing life.

I began working as a freelance writer in 1996, when I sent a half-joking article about my parents' obese and neurotic Cocker Spaniel to a dog magazine. I was at home recovering from Guillain-Barre' Syndrome, which partially paralyzed me for several months. I was pregnant with my first child, and while my husband was away during the day, I wrote. In fact, when I first gained the ability to hold a pencil again in the hospital, I grabbed the paper placemat on the dinner tray next to my hospital bed in Hahnemann

University Hospital's Acute Care Unit, and I started writing on it. I wrote about how much I missed my husband and how much I missed eating food that wasn't pureed. When I was done, the paper was all scrawled up, covered every which way, with frantic scribblings. I remember thinking, I'm a writer. It's the one thing I did when I gained the ability to use my fingers again. I couldn't even yet sit up. From that moment on, I was dedicated to writing something, anything, every day.

My first article was called, *Sam, My Fat Dog.* Really. It sounds like a children's story, because it was a joke, but friends and the magazine I sent it to, thought it was hysterical and worth something. It was about 1000 words long, and it made all the people to whom I had read it laugh, and one friend said, "You really ought to submit this to this dog magazine I subscribe to."

So, I did (I can't even remember the name of the magazine anymore, but it was a *Dog Fancy* type), and that was it. That was the beginning of it all. A few months later, I got a letter in the mail (this was before email, or at least, before I had it) and they'd accepted the piece and published it. I got $10, I think, and a free copy of the magazine. I was hooked.

I majored in English in college, but I hadn't finished yet. I dropped out my senior year to marry the most wonderful man alive. His parents were paying for his education. I was paying for mine, and I had a fairly good paying (but miserable) job with an insurance brokerage, so I decided to suspend my evening classes for a while and let him complete his teaching degree.

My professors had always given me incredibly positive feedback about my writing, and I had always planned to be a writer. Throughout my entire scholastic career, I received numerous writing awards; several at the state level. However, like most budding authors, I thought one had to rack up a lifetime of experience and degrees before they could even attempt the career. Not sure why I thought that since most journalists begin their career right out of college, or the minute they get their first assignment to cover the township debate over new speed bumps. I think it was just nerves and intimidation that made me believe that I needed to be Walter Cronkite or Ernest Hemingway before I could call myself a writer.

⇨ *We all lack self-confidence at first. Sometimes, the only cure it simply to act, to reach forward towards that long-held goal.*

In her book, *Becoming a Writer*, Dorthea Brande says, "To guarantee success, act as if it were impossible to fail. Act boldly and unseen forces will come to your aid. There are seeds of self-destruction in all of us that will bear only unhappiness if allowed to grow."

After I healed from Guillain-Barre', and I could sit up for at least five minutes at a time, I'd make my way over to my husband's ancient DOS computer, where I'd sit and write for as long as my body allowed me. I'd write stories and articles that those same poor friends had to read over and again. I thrust them on anyone who walked through the door. I'd vent about vindictive church people who told me that I must have sinned and that's why I was paralyzed. I pointed out all the reasons that was the most hateful thing I'd ever heard. There were a few of those people, and lots of those ventings. But this is how *Sam, My Fat Dog* came about, because I was bored and had something to say. That's how a lot of great writing starts. And that's where my freelancing story began.

Leonardo, my husband and I, went on to live in abject poverty and youthful stupidity for several more years. We had four beautiful children, who we fell madly in love with and who made (and still make) our lives pure joy. In between diapers and story time, walks to kindergarten and hours of PBS children's shows, I wrote. Even if I only wrote for 10 minutes or three sharp sentences that meant something only to me, I wrote.

I read everything I could about writing, and I took what I needed. Eventually, I went back to school, and while doing that, I submitted a letter to the editor of *Pennsylvania Magazine*. Someone, somewhere, advised me to "think locally" with my writing, to submit to smaller magazines and newspapers to get into the experience of freelancing. It worked. The editor emailed me back (thank God there was email at this point), and he told me that my letter had moved him greatly. He said it was an essay, and not a letter, but that he didn't have any more room in his budget to pay me for an essay, so he'd put it in the letter section, but allow it to take up the whole page.

"Front and center!" he said, "because you're a fantastic writer, and this is the best thing I've read all year."

I bought copies of the magazine and handed them out to friends and family (mostly the same people I'd been shoving things onto for years), who all looked at me strangely and said, "You realize this isn't an article, right? It's a letter to the editor."

To which I replied, "You realize that you've never been published, and I have, right? And that the editor said this was an essay and it deserved to be published? You realize *that, right?*"

I have no idea if that answer settled anything, but it allowed me to list *Pennsylvania Magazine* on my credits (which the editor insisted that I do) and submit to more magazine. From there, I wrote a travel piece about Roane Mountain State Park in Tennessee for *Country Discoveries* and a piece about Blessed Mother Teresa after her death for *St. Anthony Messenger*, and a piece about motherhood for *Canticle Magazine*. I wrote for *America Magazine* and other religious rags. I submitted a chicken barbeque recipe to *Southern Living*, which they loved (I was born in Tulsa, Oklahoma. We know barbeque). It wasn't accepted, but I received a lengthy and encouraging critique from the editor.

At the urging of a literary agent at *The Write Stuff!* Writer's Conference in Allentown, Pennsylvania, I started writing for *Associated Content*. I was averaging several hundred dollars a week writing 500 word articles on natural health and homeschooling. Editors there taught me about the importance of citing my sources, backing up my work, and marketing it to my readership. That turned into *Yahoo! Voices*, which turned into *Yahoo! News*, which turned into other magazines buying the pieces and publishing me in *Health.com* and so many other women's and natural health magazines.

I was widely quoted, I finished my bachelors, started my masters, started teaching online. I wrote two novels. They went to #1 in their Amazon categories for a time. I won some literary awards and was featured at a couple of book festivals. I sold another novel. I edited for two literary magazines and a small press. Life was full. I have continuously homeschooled, at least, one of our four children for the past 15 years, because more than one of my children have learning differences, and I wanted to be present, assisting them as they learned. So, writing is always squeezed in between life's events. I have NEVER had time for a writing retreat or a space of my own. I've always had what I call "a roaming office".

⇒**I've learned that if you want to be successful at any of the arts, you have to be persistent. I can't stress how important that is. It's the most important aspect of being an artist. It's more important than content even. Not that you can write crap, but beautifully written prose, or sharply investigated journalism will amount to exactly**

nothing if there's not a continuous workflow of submissions.

However, I discovered that, sometimes, I just wanted to do something more office oriented, something that offered me a day-to-day sharpening of my skills, but that also, could pay for all the music and art lessons my children were always involved in. Writing articles for magazines and newspapers (I was a correspondent for two local newspapers and one overseas as well) is great, but the pay is not consistent, and my family needed something more consistent. Isn't this the constant writer issue?

In all those years of building a family and a writing career, I still struggled off and on with neuromuscular issues as well. My doctors realized, once my weakness returned, that I had more than just Guillain-Barre', because the symptoms continued to return in a wax-and-wane sort of fashion. I sometimes was in a wheelchair and sometimes I worked my way up to a cane when, whatever it was I had, would rear its ugly head again. After several horrible neurologists, I finally found one that paid attention, and it was discovered that I had Myasthenia Gravis. With four children and a busy life, I knew that I couldn't work full-time, and I doubted that any of the freelance services I been told about would be worth the effort. But at the urging of the same literary agent who'd suggested *Associated Content*, I paid for a $10 account with Elance, and figured that I might be able to accrue enough money to pay for the account, at least, so that it wasn't a total loss. There was that doubt again, but I knew enough to just let it babble on in the background and not let it stop me from moving forward.

I watched all the Elance tutorials, took all the online advice offered by the staff at Elance, and submitted one proposal at a time, and then, waited. Nothing happened. For a full week, nothing happened at all. Every job rejected me. I was infuriated and humiliated. I was a published author! I had been paid (in peanuts, mostly, but still paid) for my work! What were these people missing? What was I missing? So I got angry and submitted five articles every day for five days. By the end of the week, I had 10 offers and had to turn all but three tiny jobs down. I wanted to see how this whole thing worked before I committed completely.

I loved all three jobs. They were quirky and quick. They didn't pay much, at first, but every client was wonderful to work with, and one is my friend to this day. From there, I gained more clients, and I had steady work for a long time. I uploaded the Elance app to my phone, so that I could talk to clients when I was waiting in the school parking lot, stuck in a pediatrician's waiting room, or behind a couponer at the grocery store.

When I needed Immunoglobulin treatments or kidney surgery, I let the current jobs wind down and didn't accept any more until I needed more. Clients were always understanding at Elance and, because I timed things right, I had the space to take time off.

It's really that simple. Along the way, I have led many people to Elance (which is now Upwork), Guru, Fiverr, and other places, where they have made successful freelance careers for themselves. All of them have outpaced me, because I simply cannot do the physical work that they can, but I love this work, and if you like working for yourself, creating your own schedule, controlling your income, you'll probably love this too. I quickly went from a nobody on Elance/Upwork to a routinely featured freelancer. Elance and Upwork marketed my services to thousands of their clients on a daily basis on the front page of their website. It's not hard to get here. It just takes some good, persistent work.

Thank you for taking the time to read my story. See, I had a lot of the same questions and misgivings that you probably do, but I didn't have anyone to reassure me that any of this was a good idea. I guess I was just too dumb to doubt. I had faith in myself and in God to lead me to the next viable opportunity. He always does. He makes a way, lays down a lighted path each day. I don't want to turn this into a preaching book, but faith is a centerpiece of my life, and it's one of the key ingredients to my motivation. The other two are finances and the pure addiction of writing. I have a love for writing stronger than I do for most other things, so I know that even if I wasn't getting paid, I'd still be writing. Now that there's speech-to-text software, even if my fingers stopped working again, I'd be writing. I know that some of you are like that as well. You're a good fit for the freelancing life. For those of you who love writing, but who still find that you must drudge up motivation each day, don't count yourself out just yet. You might find that your first freelancing job turns you into a short-article-writing-addict after all.

Now it's time to learn some valuable freelancing tips, so you can start writing your own freelance story.

WRAP-UP

- **You can begin this work with just a knack for great writing**

- **You must be persistent**

- **You must believe in yourself**

- **Even with a disability, a family, relationship, etc...You can make this work.**

- **This life is up to you, no one else.**

Chapter Two

Banish Doubt

**"Faith and doubt cannot exist in the same mind
and the same time, for one will dispel the other."
Thomas S. Monson**

When I began writing this book I asked some
friends what their biggest doubts were in regards to
making a living as a freelance writer for online
services. Several of them were beginning their
freelance careers, several more were not writers at all
and were interested in this kind of career but didn't
know how to go about achieving it, and several more
had attempted it, but gave up almost immediately.
Why? I wanted to know. What I discovered is that the
biggest fear that emerging freelance writers have is
this:

*Am I good enough to get clients to believe in my
work?* And *If I get clients, am I good enough to get hired
continuously?*

I offer a resounding YES to both questions. If
you're reading this book, you're already someone who's
interested in writing, or you have been a writer for
many years. Maybe you self-published a few novels,
had several short stories published, or maybe, you just
like to write and you've got a good sense of customer
service. If you can write, you have organizational skills
(or can quickly develop them), and you remain
consistent, you will find clients who regularly want
your work. The key is to submit constantly and
produce excellent work. There is such a plethora of
continuous work at sites like Upwork that there are
really not enough workers to go around. So, any writer
for these services has the advantage. You are

needed...in spades! There is a demand for the kind of writing you do--whether it is creative, nonfiction health articles, content fillers for blogs and websites, marketing materials, fashion and/music reviews, curriculum writing, etc...There is work, and you need work, so do good work, remain consistent, and believe in yourself--even just a little bit. A mustard seed's worth of self-confidence will do, and the mustard seed is the smallest seed in the world, but it still grows a huge plant that spreads. A little confidence can work that same way for your writing career.

The problem that I find with so many emerging freelancers is that they submit one or two proposals a week and then sit around sad and despondent waiting for responses from potential customers. You simply can't do that when you're freelancing. Basic physics tell us that we must remain in motion to maintain our balance. A successful freelancing career is a constantly moving wheel, just as all self-employment is. If you aren't constantly putting your work and ideas out there for potential clients to review, you won't have any work. Your work/life balance is off. You'll have an excessive amount of time to navel gaze and feel sorry for yourself, but you won't be working.

A successful freelancer doesn't sit on her hands. She's busy typing all day. A successful freelancer submits, at least, five proposals a day for five days. I call this the "5 for 5 Method". This is where you create several high-quality, but diversified, proposals that can apply to several different fields and skill sets and you submit AT LEAST five of these a day for an entire work week, whatever your work week is. You take the weekends off, and you don't think about who is or isn't reviewing your proposals. You move blindly ahead until you get an offer, pressing that work forward, peddling that bicycle. You continuously look for more work. You submit, submit, submit, and you don't stop submitting until you have enough work to keep you afloat for as long as you need it. When those jobs run out...actually, before those jobs run out, you begin the submission process all over again. Something important to note about freelancing, YOU create the balance. Life does not present balance for you. It only creates circumstances, and it's up to you to rearrange them according to your needs. You simply cannot expect to keep working if you're not, well, working. So, if you aren't regularly sending out new proposals each morning, you're not getting jobs regularly each morning, or each new week. This process must continue. It can't slow, or your work will slow.

Now, not every freelancer is a full-time freelancer. Sometimes, the work is part-time, or as needed. If this is the case, you can loosen up the submission process a bit. You aren't relying on work from online freelance services to pay for your bread and butter, so you can approach things a bit less aggressively, but you would still apply the same sort of consistency. If you want to make, say, $300 a week freelancing, but you only want easy non-stressful jobs, then you'll need about three different jobs.

First, you'll apply the "5 for 5 Method" until you get, maybe, three small jobs. Say you take a job blogging about carpet care and replacement for a carpet installation company every week, one blogging about wedding etiquette for a wedding boutique, and one writing a weekly business article for a start-up business magazine. These are all examples of small writing jobs I've done through Upwork. Each of these jobs you can do with some basic research and guidance from the client.

You set up the hours you're going to work, and you agree on a due date, or milestone. Done. If another client invites you to do an additional job for them during that time, you'll simply turn down that offer, because you already have a full plate. However, you know that these jobs are not all long term. Maybe the wedding boutique one is and the start-up magazine is, but the carpet installation company won't need your help forever. So, as you near the end of that job, you apply the "5 for 5 Method" until you get that job replaced with a new one of similar time constraint and complexity. You're an expert freelancer by now, and have several high ratings, so you know that you're going to get more than one offer. You turn down all that don't work for you, and you move on. It's really that simple.

⇨**You can be an excellent, successful freelance writer online by simply creating great work and being consistent with the submission process. If you learn nothing else from this book, at least, walk away with that knowledge in your mind.**

Veteran freelance editor and proofreader at *Nicean Magazine,* Little Flower Press, and Booktrope Publishing, Elaine Papciak, asked the question in one of my webinars once, "How does one balance working full-time and freelancing on the side? It's hard to do!"

My response was simple:

"Yeah, it is hard to do sometimes. You have to meet your physical needs first. If that's done through your full-time job, tend to that job before you even worry about your freelancing work. Set aside an evening, or an afternoon, when you are not working your full-time job and can enjoy your freelancing. If freelancing is always your 'on the side' job, don't ever sweat it, and walk away for a bit if it gets to be too much. Don't sacrifice your sleep for that. The work will be there when you're ready to come back to it."

A similar truth applies to those who freelance full-time. Remember to meet your physical needs first. If you're not yet employed as a freelancer, get your membership with as many online freelancing services as you can afford. Memberships are usually about

$10-$20 a month. Pay for the membership. A free membership will get you nowhere. I know what I'm talking about.

I didn't land any viable jobs until I paid for the membership. I don't know if these services hide the view of good jobs, or clients with verified payments already in place, or what, but I just know from my personal experience and many others' that if you go with the free membership you'll get squat for jobs. True story. Don't be cheap (but that's for another chapter).

Get your paid membership, set aside the time during the day when you plan to have office hours, and submit that entire time. This is even more aggressive than the "5 for 5 Method", but if you've got mortgage or rent due and you're hungry, this is the method you're really going to need. Meet your physical needs first. Spending eight hours a day submitting all day long will get you jobs quickly and get you enough jobs to pay your bills. But don't sit there sweating and fretting all day. That will also come out in your proposals. Potential clients will smell that fear and leave you sitting there forever. Take pride in your skills. You know you have them, or you wouldn't be reading this book. People have told you that you're a great writer. You've told yourself that before, even if you've spent most of your writing life trying to talk yourself out of taking a decent risk. Lean on that logical part of your brain that says,

"Look, pal, you write well. I've seen it. Others have seen it. You like writing. It makes your heart slow down. It makes your palms sweat less. It's therapeutic. Even writing a concise and efficient email makes you feel more like yourself. You got this. There are a million jobs at Upwork alone. Relax. Submit proposals and relax. The work will come to you."

Yeah, listen to the smarter part of yourself, not the vindictive part that comes from all the negative people you've known in your life.

⇨**Negativity has no fit in the freelancing life. It will ruin it, eat it up from the inside out.**

Don't let it do that to you. Wave it away like a bad smell. Lock it up like the dangerous enemy it is, and move forward. Get up, get back on the bike, and start pedaling. Even if you're shaky at first, even if you fall once or twice, get up and keep moving. Even if you didn't ever learn to ride a bike or swim, I can promise you, that you would have stayed on balance or kept afloat if you'd just kept moving. Babies and dogs know this when they first hit the water. You don't have to teach either to swim. We humans only forget how to swim when we're taught to fear the water. Stop listening to fear. Statistics of failure will always be around you. Around the whole world, all the time, because failure happens. But failure is not the same thing as a mistake. Mistakes are really lessons. They happen so that we can learn how to better get back into the water or better get back up on the bike and keep moving forward. So you fell once? So you fell twice? Who gives a rip? Stop focusing on the job you almost had and start working towards the one that will pay that electric bill that's looming in big yellow "CANCELLATION" letters. Do it now.

And before you say, "Well, it's easy for her to say that. She's an experienced freelancer already."

Look, I've lived without heat and hot water before I began freelancing. I've lost my electricity and a home to a short sale before I discovered the art of writing for online freelance services. I was born into serious poverty. I know what it feels like to be desperate. I once ran out of formula for my baby and pay day was a week away. All I had was half and half left over from some snotty church ladies who dropped by my house to tell me that they hoped I'd finally "gotten saved" out of my Catholic faith. Thank God for that half and half and those church ladies. If I hadn't had something of substance to give my baby he might have starved to death, and thank God those church ladies were so snotty. Had been anything other than a natural writer, I would have lashed out at them with in-person words. Instead, I wrote my anger out. I used that gumption to sit down and start writing and submitting to multiple magazines at once. I found my voice, and I found that other people shared it.

Circumstances had been placed before me by life. I took them back and rearranged them. I leaned on my abilities and the faith that raised me and taught me that there is always something bigger than us that is looking out for our good.

Poverty is, indeed, the master of invention and it, along with other difficult circumstances, can make you want to get back on that bike and make a living out of your good writing. Guillain-Barre' Syndrome did that for me as well. It made me itchy to write. You need that kind of itch to be successful at anything, really. You need the desire for hard work. You need the payoff, too.

So, yeah, I know what it's like to be poor and be a writer. I know what it's like to have to bet my paycheck on the amount of submissions I send out, and I can tell you that faith, consistency, and good work will yield good results, my friend. Don't give up on yourself. Believe in you.

Check out the "community" sections of all of these sites, as well. There, you can find other freelancers with questions similar to yours. You can begin conversations there and get quick answers to any problems you are having as well. For additional information about getting health insurance, and other necessities generally granted to traditionally employed people, check out the National Writers Union and the Freelancer's Union. You can get some really good information and resources there to help make your full-time freelancing career even more stable.

WRAP-UP

- Get rid of negativity. It is not your friend.
- Create continuous good work.
- Persistence is more important than anything else.
- Connect with other freelancers through other communities, like the Freelancer's Union and communities set up on sites like Upwork and others.

CHAPTER THREE

Using Online Freelance Services like Upwork, Guru,
Fiverr and Others

"It's hard to beat a person who never gives up."
Babe Ruth

Before you log onto any freelance service sites, like
Upwork or Guru, decide what kind of job you want to
do. Peruse their available jobs, and make a list of what
you will and will not do. Be aware that for as many
people who say they are in love with this kind of work
and these sites, there will be 10 people who never got
the hang of it, failed, and call all of them a scam.
They're not scams. They're legitimate employment
agencies. You can find continuous, meaningful, and
well-paying work here, but you have to work. That's
the key, and you have to know what you want.

Get a notebook. Any notebook. A Dollar Store wide-
ruled, one subject, will do. Write "Freelancing Jobs" on
the cover. Open to the first page and title it "Dream
Jobs". Make a list of as many writing dream jobs as
you can think of. Whether it's fiction or non-fiction
writing you want, make the list. It doesn't matter how
outlandish it sounds, because there are so many jobs
at Upwork alone that you are sure to find that dream
job there several times over. As long as the client has a
decent review rating, and their payment has been
verified, it's a legitimate job.

You'll have to download a time tracker app that will
allow your client to see what kind of work you've done
and how many hours you were actually working on it.
Or, you'll be paid via milestones. In other words, you'll
have a set time that your work is supposed to be
finished. You might have one big milestone; your
project might be small and is due in a week. Only one

milestone is needed. Your work might be lengthy, and you'll reach a milestone every Friday evening at midnight. It just depends on the job and the work requirements, but all jobs have time trackers and/or milestone measurements, and with a time tracker your work day gets screenshot in random intervals. So no Facebooking! (That's also for another chapter).

I have written fiction eBooks for clients. I have written textbooks on writing for a small college in the United Kingdom. I've edited romance novels and thrillers. I've proofread multiple books on natural health. I've created high-quality, long term, investigative journalism pieces for an American expat magazine in St. Petersburg, Russia. There are so many jobs at sites like Upwork and Guru, that you can really find that dream job. So, write it down and keep the list handy. You'll want to aim for these jobs. You'll want to filter your search to find them.

The same principle applies to making a list of jobs you refuse to do. Think about why you'd never do them, and write that down next to the job title, because if you won't ghostwrite a romance novel, because you're uncomfortable writing about sex, then this is important to note. You might be invited to write something about natural health one day and there might be a section on healthy sex. You'll want to find out ahead of time what your chapters are going to cover. Having that list will help you to remember that you need to get ALL THE DETAILS before you begin a long term ghostwriting project.

Having the "I Won't Ever Do This!" list will also help you to better manage your time. Maybe you won't ever work for a client who demands 24 hour attention. If you suspect that this kind of client is showing up in the first description of the job, you'll remember your promise to yourself and you won't take this job. There will be another job. There always is. Freelancing is never going to go away. Keep your standards. Respect yourself. And you'll find that you'll continue to love your work.

Freelancer, Dr. Thaeda Franz says, "Don't expect to be paid what you are worth until you have a loyal following. You will be paid what the market allows-regardless of your credentials. Once you have several good reviews, you might be able to charge more than most- but at the start, you have to be willing to take less money to get jobs and be able to prove you are worth the big bucks...As an example, I have a PhD in psychology and generally would like to charge at least $50/hr for my time- right now. Given that I have only worked on a few contracts, I can only charge half that."

The easiest way to do that is to take small jobs at first, for a very short time. Treat them like an internship, because this is exactly what they are. You'll learn how to interact well with clients, the social etiquette for online business, and how to quickly produce quality work. Clients are often willing to offer advice and feedback as well. Always end each job thanking your client for the opportunity to work for them (even if you found them or the job difficult at times), and ask for a public review and some personal feedback. Ask, "Is there anything I could have done better?" They'll tell you, and when they do, write it down in a "Notes from Clients" notebook. You'll want to refer to it later.

WRAP-UP

- Be willing to take tiny jobs for little pay when you first start. Just the first three or four jobs. This will build up your high ratings and reviews and, after that, you can get any jobs you want.
- Make a list of Dream Jobs and things you Won't Do.

- Online freelance services are pools of talent and potential clients looking to make a synergistic, short or long term business exchange.

- They seek your talent. You accept, sign the contract, and get the job.
- You get paid through milestones and/or hourly online verified time trackers.
- The money from your client goes into escrow, so you are guaranteed to be paid for your work.
- DO NOT accept work from a client whose payment has not been verified.
- DO NOT accept work from a client who doesn't have any reviews.

CHAPTER FOUR

Creating Proposals with a Hook

"Creativity comes from trust. Trust your instincts and never hope more than you work."
Rita Mae Brown

In freelance writing online, you are your proposal. The strength of the job proposal you send to your potential client is key to landing the job. This seems obvious, but you'd be surprised how many new freelancers, either, lazily breeze through the submission process or over-obsess so that the whole piece sounds like an ode to Victor Hugo and not a proposal for how a 300-word article on healthy cat food is going to get written. So, it's important to make the proposal short and sweet, but sharper than what everyone else is doing.

Create three different proposals that show off your specific skills. These will be proposals for three different kinds of jobs, not three different proposals for the same job. Having this diversity will allow you to submit for several similar, but still different, writing jobs all in the same day.

Employers and recruiters (this works for all kinds of work, even in-person, non-writing, jobs) routinely scan resumes for certain keywords. Find out what yours need to be. If you are looking for copywriting work, that exact word needs to be in your resume'. So does "editing," "content writing," "English Literature," and/or "Communications."

If you're looking for a job writing articles for a business' website, you need words like "copy," "marketing," "SEO, (search engine optimization), and the actual word "keyword". I will go into more detail on each of these words, what they really mean in the "online sense" and how to make them work for you.

For example, if you are a creative writer, make a proposal template listing those skills and what you can do with them. If you have extensive experience in editing academic papers, create a proposal for that. If you're an English teacher, create an educational proposal template. There's a lot of freelance work for teachers--curriculum writers (I've written chapters in two textbooks).

Always put your links in your proposals and offer to write a brief 200 word sample piece pertaining to their job posting. Always address the client as personally as possible--using their name if it is available. If it's not, then simply begin by telling them why you'd be excited to take on this job for them. Don't take jobs you wouldn't be thrilled about, that wouldn't drag you out of bed in the morning. If you're going to hate it, save everyone's time (yours, the client's) and just keep looking until you find something that sounds interesting. If you like constant change, choose short term jobs only. Remember, you're in charge. It's your career. You own it when you're a freelancer.

Build a strong portfolio of work before you begin. This can be academic papers you wrote, samples from eBooks you've published, other articles you've written and ghostwritten, blog links, etc...Wherever you can show off your skills, do so in your portfolio, so that potential clients can see what you can do for them. If you don't have a strong portfolio yet, create one. Start a blog and post something. Invite your friends to comment on it. Don't get distracted by making the perfect blog. You're just creating a place where potential clients can view your work. Or make up mock blog posts, ones that you would write if you had a blog, and put those in your online portfolio on whatever freelancing site(s) you use.

Learn something about SEO and Keywords. SEO stands for Search Engine Optimization. It simply means using the best words possible in your articles and online work to draw the most readers to your page through search engines like Google, Explorer, or Bing. Google, hands down, offers the best method to search for anything on the internet. Your clients will, most likely, want you to know as much about Google searches as you can learn. The best advice for research here is to simple Google the acronym "SEO" and learn everything that you can. There are whole books and sections of Barnes and Nobles about it. Better yet, search your local independent bookstore to find out everything you can.

I'm not going to get into it too deeply in this book, because it's a whole other book, but do your research. Nothing about SEO is complicated. Some people will argue against that, but it's just not true. You can learn what you need about SEO pretty quickly in order to help someone beef up the searchers and readers being brought to her/his site.

Keywords are those "key words" that you use in an article, an article title, via tagging and categories, to draw readers to your site. This is the other side of SEO. If you're writing that article about how to know when you need to throw out that old carpet versus having it cleaned, you might use the keywords "carpet", "when to throw out your old carpet", "name of carpet company," and "the best carpet cleaner in the United States", etc...You'll use the words most likely to draw readers to your site. You can only use so many keywords in so many words, like four keywords in 1100 words (or something like that), before Google or Facebook registers the article as spam. So, learn the ratio and follow it. Your client may have it written into the contract, but he may not either, so Google it. You'll find the answers you need quickly.

Learning to research on a second's notice and create an outstanding 500-word-article in an afternoon is a common occurrence for freelancers. Get used to that kind of movement. Dr. Thaeda Franz notes, "Be willing/able to work fast. There is plenty of work out there, but many potential employers want rapid turnaround (24-48 hours)."

Do an exercise here. Just for fun. Pretend you're writing a blog post about wedding etiquette in the South for that wedding boutique blog. What keywords might you use if the client has told you that, while you're talking about child's etiquette in your blog post, you're really selling flower girl dresses and ring bearer tuxedos that are sold at the boutique's website? You have to research children's etiquette at a traditional Southern American wedding, but your keywords would have to be something like this: American Southern wedding etiquette, flower girl dresses, name of boutique, ring bearer suits, tuxedos, weddings in America, American weddings, etc...Do you get the idea? On the surface, the article is about etiquette, but it's really just selling the clothes on your client's website.

Remember that the same kind of writer "rules" apply to freelancing articles about watches as it does for writing fiction. There must be a hook to everything--a hook to your proposal (what makes you so special?), a hook to your article or product description. If you're writing an article, there should be a hook, a middle, and a closing that wraps everything up. Read some well written articles online if you want to see how it's done. Go to blogs and places where you might find articles written in the way your client will ask you to write them. BUT MAKE EVERYTHING YOUR OWN! Do not plagiarize! Do not say that someone else's work is yours, or that your work is someone else's. Don't fail to cite your sources. Your client can take any citations away if they so choose. If you're ghostwriting an article, you'll keep a copy of your piece for future samples and portfolio pieces, but once it's published by your client, the rights all belong to them. It's on them in every way, but before you submit that article or blog post, cite anything that needs citing. Want to learn more about the *Chicago Manual of Style, APA*, or *MLA*? Go to Purdue OWL. Google it. You'll find everything you need there.

⇒ **Word counts matter! If your client says they only want you writing an article that is 500 words, then you can't write 499 or 501. You won't get paid. You must write a 500 word article. This is very important to remember.**

⇒ **Try this:**

Write a 200 word product description for a baby stroller. Did it have a hook? Was it within the word count EXACTLY? And would their keywords draw readers to their client's site?

WRAP UP

- Create proposals with a hook by immediately addressing your client's needs in the first line.

- Share only your relevant education and experience.

- List the skills that relate to the job at hand.

- Be KIND! Thank the potential client for taking the time to review your proposal and sample work.

- Offer a very brief sample piece and refer client to your portfolio.

- Make your portfolio shine.

- Learn about keywords, SEO, and word counts.

CHAPTER FIVE

Let Your Passion Show!

"You can do anything as long as you have the passion, the drive, the focus, and the support."

Sabrina Bryant

There are enough jobs on freelance service sites to go around. Literally, hundreds of thousands of new ones are posted each day across these sites. Find the ones you love, even the low-paying ones to gain ratings and a reputation. Begin your proposal by saying why you'd "love to take on this job" or why you're passionate about coding, natural health articles, or early childhood education. Whatever the job is, make sure it's somewhere near or on your Dream Job list. You will find it hard to sleep at night this way, because you'll be excited to start work the next day, and you'll find that you love going out to the coffee house to get a big mocha java to sit down for a few hours and work the project your new client in Australia just gave you.

PASSION SELLS! If you're a slug, no one will want you. You'll look just like all the other slugs begging for a writing job. Smile through your words! Sell your joy, and you'll get the job. You're sending out five proposals a day, anyway. You'll start to get even feedback on those proposals for jobs that you don't get. You'll get messages from potential clients who have future work for you.

Write your proposal in this order: Address the details of the job in one or two sentences and how you're an expert in this area, or how you're well-versed in this detail or that one. Add relative experience and education. Only relative. Don't tell them about your Bachelors of Fine Arts if they're hiring you for your Masters in English Education. It's not relative. Offer to send the potential client a short, 200 word (at most! Don't send your work away for free!) sample of your writing, or whatever applies to your genre of work, and tell them that the links to your online work are below, your best portfolio pieces are attached. Tell them how hard you're going to work for them, how adept you are at following deadlines, and thank them for taking the time to read your work. Tell them that you're looking forward to hearing from them and working with them. Wish them a great day.

⇨ **BE KIND! No one is really doing this on a day-to-day basis in the freelancing world.**

Be that change, the kindness you wish to see, and sincerely thank them for investing a few moments in your proposal and wish them a wonderful day. Trust me, they'll remember you for this. Gratefulness equals success in the freelancing world. It will make you and your client much happier. Be honest. Don't lie about your skills, education, or abilities. You don't have to be superman when you know what you're good at and what you're not good at. You only have to be yourself. If you're good at writing health articles, then seek out health articles. If you're good at blogging about mom issues, then search jobs about blogging for mothers. If you're fluent in Farsi, then look for jobs writing product descriptions in Farsi. Be honest and kind, and you will go far. Get bitter and hold grudges and you'll spin out before you start.

And that brings me to another point---GET A DECENT PORTFOLIO SET UP! Get a professional looking photo set up even if it's a snapshot from your phone. It can't be an amateurish photo. Would you go on a first date with ketchup smeared in your hair and smelling like a horse stall? No, you wouldn't. So, don't go to a proposal with a picture of you on a Disneyworld trip with the family or heavy-lidded from a hangover. Get a decent photo and add portfolio items to your profile that potential clients can readily check out. Impress them! Also, make your portfolio visible for clients to view. Don't make it private. You can make your personal information and profile invisible to internet searches if you like, however. This is helpful if you write in other places under a pen name. This separates your freelancing life from your fiction writing or literary life.

Wrap UP

- Take on projects that you're passionate about.

- Create a decent profile that's inviting to clients.

- Get a professional photo, or professional looking photo.

- Make your profile visible to potential clients, while still protecting it from outside-the-company viewers if you wish.

CHAPTER SIX

Be Persistent

"Nothing in this world can take the place of persistence. Talent will not: nothing is more common than unsuccessful men with talent. Genius will not; unrewarded genius is almost a proverb. Education will not: the world is full of educated derelicts. Persistence and determination alone are omnipotent."

Calvin Coolidge

It takes real effort to be a regularly discouraged person. In fact, it takes as much effort to consistently give up as it does to consistently get up. Persistence is the most important aspect of succeeding as a freelance writer online. It is the key to everything. You absolutely cannot get tired. Even if you are tired, you can't give into the fatigue of submitting and resubmitting and submitting some more. You must apply, at least, the "5 for 5 Method" where you submit five proposals a day for five days (taking the weekends off). Without this kind of consistent effort, you will yield nothing more than some phishing scams that do, occasionally, make their way through services like Upwork and Guru.

Even if you only excel in one area of writing, like article--writing, blogging, technical writing, technology writing (not the same thing as technical writing), continuous content, SEO, keyword marketing, etc...It is the **consistency that will make you successful at your career,** not the content. Yes, you read that right. Let's repeat it:

⇨ **It's the consistency of your submission process that will make you successful at your freelancing career, not the content.**

Explanation needed? Are you shaking your head? "But I have an MFA! I have a degree in Comparative Literature from Harvard University! The content indeed matters!" Well, it's true that if you write crap no one is going to want to hire you again, you'll get bad ratings, and your time at Upwork will be over. However, if you write decently, are willing to hone your craft, take direction, put your client first, and *CONSISTENTLY SUBMIT AND RESUBMIT* you will have consistent, viable, work that will pay your bills.

The number one key to being a successful freelancer through services like Upwork, is to apply the "5 For 5 Method" and continue to submit until you get enough jobs to keep you going fulltime, part-time, or whatever it is that you need financially. You will be able to remove yourself from a job proposal if you land other jobs in the meantime. And you will have to do this every time you need a new batch of jobs. I tend to work for several months, take a month off and take care of family and personal issues, work on my fiction writing, graduate school work, etc...But when I return to work, I need a new set of clients. So, I send out proposals all over again, using the "5 For 5 Method", and regain all the hours and income I need.

Myasthenia Gravis keeps me from working as a freelancer full time. I could easily do it, but I curtail my work so that I have time to take care of me when I need IV treatments or just time for rest. You can do this even if you're disabled. That's the beauty of the freelance life.

I know that I've already said much of this in prior chapters, but I cannot emphasize the importance of persistence, so let me repeat...BE CONSISTENT. SUBMIT WELL AND SUBMIT OFTEN.

Wrap UP

- **Submit, submit, submit**

- **Be persistent**

- **Persistence is more important than even content**

CHAPTER SEVEN

DO GOOD WORK!

"Be a yardstick of quality. Some people aren't used to an environment where excellence is accepted."

Steve Jobs

Don't half-step, don't cut corners, don't lie, and don't cheat. All of that is robbing your client of the work they're paying for and the life and freedom you are trying to create for yourself. Be honest. If you start a job for someone, end it with them on good terms. You do not want a client giving you bad reviews.

Set up regular work hours and sit down every day to submit more proposals or to do your work, if you have some. Whatever you promise your client you will do, do it. If some kind of family emergency comes along, inform them as quickly as possible. Don't wait until the last minute. You don't want any bad reviews. Reviews are what make your career. Of course, your client doesn't want any bad reviews either, or they'll be without decent freelancers to get their work done, but you have more to lose than they do.

If you have to end a job early, do it as kindly and politely as you can. This sounds so obvious that it seems moronic, but I can promise you that when you're caught in the midst of a complicated job that simply can't be finished in the way your demanding client wants it done, you're going to have to fall on your sword. You're going to have to take the blame, don't become defensive, and offer to forgo the next upcoming milestone payment, or whatever "giveaway" you can come up with. If you're breaking a contract, do it for excellent reasons, don't do it more than once in a two year period, and take the blame for the fall. Sometimes, the best you can hope for is to walk away without a bad review. No review is not a bad review if you already have a slew of high reviews. Just try to put yourself in the client's shoes. They've hired you to do a job they can't do or that they don't have the time to do.

I once had to end a job early with a client who lived across the ocean. I've had a lot of clients who live in other countries. This client was actually wonderful. He was nice and thoughtful. He had only kind things to say, but his terms didn't match his contract. They changed constantly. He wanted Skype meetings with me, but he was in Istanbul. I told him that I could get up at 5am my time to work with him, but no earlier. He'd consistently call at 1am and get upset that I wasn't around at the agreed upon time. When I tried to explain to him that we'd agreed on 5am EST, he said he understood, apologized, and it happened all over again the next day for several days. Then, after I finally sent him some back and forth questions, got the four articles written that he'd requested, he said he wanted me to have them published at magazines where I didn't even have privilege. He was a fairly important person in his community, and I know that he really did think that contracts worked this way, that they were pretty fluid, but I still couldn't work this way. So, I offered him the four articles for free and told him that he was free to have them published wherever he wanted. I told him that I couldn't really comply with his changing terms. He didn't argue. He took the work and moved on. He was upset, and feared that he'd not find anyone else to have his work published elsewhere, but I did eventually see one of the articles on Buzz Feed, so I know that he got something done. In the end, he gave me a nice review for having worked hard to meet his needs. Sometimes, weird stuff happens when you're freelancing. If you remember to be kind along the way, it's just weird. If you're rude and defensive, it can be the end of your career.

Apply the same kind of vigorous quality and editing skills to your blogging and article writing that you did when you were writing a short story for your BFA. Treat every single job as though it's the only one you have even if you have three at one time. Focus is very important in freelancing. Focus on the work at hand before you work on the next item. In other words, if you're working for two clients at a time, work half the day for one and half for the other, and when you're working for one, don't think constantly about the other.

Wrap Up

- **Sometimes weird stuff happens in freelancing.**

- **But if you're kind, you'll always end up on top.**

- **Put yourself in your client's shoes.**

- **Do good work.**

- **Focus on one job at a time even if you're working multiple jobs within a pay period.**

CHAPTER EIGHT

Get Organized

"...*organizing your space is just a matter of aligning your stuff to your future.*"

Colleen Warmingham, Minimoligist: Organize, Reclaim, Emerge.

Get organized. This will save your life. My dear friend and professional organizer, Colleen Warmingham, is fond of saying that it's not really about things. Organizing is about hopes and dreams and the things we hold on to. Often times, when you're having trouble getting work done on time, you're procrastinating, or you're unduly stressed while working on a certain freelancing job, it's because it's not the right job for you. This could be for a myriad of reasons.

Perhaps, you chose this job, because your family needs more money and the client invited you to do the work. It was money, so you accepted it, but that doesn't mean you should have. This is where you refer to your "Dream List" and the list of jobs you won't do. If you're sketchy about a job when it's offered to you, look over both lists. Does it violate any of the boundaries you've set for yourself as a freelancer? Then don't take the job. If you're already stuck in it, complete the next milestone and get out of the job as soon as you can. Refer to the last chapter on how to break contracts if ABSOLUTELY necessary. If it isn't absolutely necessary, use this bad job as a teaching experience about what you won't do. Add it to your list.

⇒ Get a calendar and use it.

It doesn't have to be an expensive, fancy one. It just has to be one that works for you. I always have a dry erase board above my desk, where I have a list of current clients and the days that milestones are due, or the hours required and agreed upon to complete the job. Some freelancers find that it's easier to use a spreadsheet. Whatever works for you, do that. Just get a calendar that has room to list the daily work you'll be doing for each of your clients. In short order, you will find out how much work you can handle in one day, one week.

⇒ Create a clean workspace.

I'm a messy creative. I "get" that sometimes your art gets plastered everywhere during the creative process, but freelancing is not one of the places where you can do this and still be successful. Yes, you can lean on the skills you learned in art school to be the best freelancer possible, but your desk should be clean and set up in a way that works for you. If that means you live out of piles that are accessible, then fine. But that rarely works when you're freelancing full-time. It's better to get filing cabinets and arrange work by order of months, keep contact lists for your clients--past and present, because you may want to contact them later to find more work, and make sure that the family, your partner, any roommates, etc...Know that you have this space set aside for your work.

I find that it's helpful to make phone calls and send emails first thing in the morning. Even though I've used an online time tracker in the past, I will still message my client periodically throughout the work process to tell them where I am in it and how much I've gotten done that day. If they don't want to know any of this, they'll tell you. If they are new to Upwork or other freelancing services, they'll so appreciate that you're pulling them out of the dark. Explain any processes they don't understand. Lead them to the online community for whatever service you use if they have questions you can't answer about the system, payments, or anything else you don't feel expert enough to speak to.

I once had a wonderful client from Knoxville, Tennessee who hired me to write a series of continuous small business articles for a newsletter he was launching in the Smoky Mountain region. He gave me the subject matter. I did any research necessary, and I wrote the articles at a regular pace for him. He set up milestones for me, but he wasn't sure how to send payments from his end, so he asked me for help. I told him that I had no idea how this was done and I sent him to someone in accounts who handled this sort of thing. It took him a while, but he eventually figured it out, and he gave me a glowing review, because I was patient and I sent him where he needed to go.

As a freelancer, you're coming aboard one, or more, of these services as an expert in your area or as someone who's willing to learn how to become an expert. Remember that the person who's hiring you is depending on you to have the answers to his/her questions or to be willing to do the research, even research on how to pay you, if necessary. Just be persistent and kind, and you'll do well. I know both of these are repeats, but I can't repeat persistence and kindness enough. It will make you good at all you do.

⇨Create Office Hours

Let your client know when you will be available during the day. If the job you've accepted says that you need to be available immediately, whenever your client contacts you, and you're okay with that, go with it. If you're not okay with that, make that clear at the beginning. If your client doesn't say anything about office hours, kindly let them know when you accept the job that you are generally available from 9am-5pm and again from 7pm-10pm, Mon-Sat, or whatever your schedule is.

Sometimes, clients will require specific hour time slots and you'll have to abide by that if you agree to the contract. The online time tracker (and, by the way, whatever service you go with will prompt you to download it) will show your client that you've kept these hours. But most of the time, your client will not require this, and you will have to rely on your own created work hours to keep the workflow going. I can tell you that if you sit down at the same time every day, even on the days when you don't want to work, you will begin working. That consistent set-up and routine will form a habit. And what are habits but those things that we create to compensate for our own laziness. Remember, you're a freelancer. You can work in your pajamas and refuse to brush your hair for a week. So you're going to have to create habits that will sustain that previously spoken of balance. Create a habit of work hours that will propel you out of bed and into that plush leather desk seat of yours (or onto the couch next to the bag of Cheetos where you do your best freelancing work).

Wrap Up

- **Get organized.**

- **Get a calendar and respect deadlines.**

- **Be kind!**

- **Be persistent!**

- **Be willing to send your client to support services if he/she asks a question you can't answer about getting paid, how to open files, or anything else.**

- **Create office hours or abide by the office hours that you and your client have agreed upon.**

- **Create a habit of working consistently and hard at the same time every day. You'll do well.**

CHAPTER NINE

FOLLOW UP WITH PAST CLIENTS

"No matter how busy you are, you must take the time to make the other person feel important."

Mary Kay Ash

I worked for a client for more than a year on a weekly article series for several of his websites. I loved it. It was wonderful work, and after an introductory price of $9 for every 1000 word article (this was years ago and that was a going rate), he gave me a generous raise and I was making $15 for every 1000 word article, and I wrote three to four articles a day for him. When our year together ended, I took some time off. I had three other clients as well. All those jobs sort of fizzled out on their own, and I took a month vacation. When the vacation was over, however, I decided to check in with all of them and see if there was anything new for them that I might be able to do. They all had more work for me, and I began up again.

Not only did I have more work from each of these clients, but the first client, the one who'd given me my first raise, suggested an online teaching company he'd help found. He discovered that I had a degree in Education, as well as a strong writing background, and he asked if I'd be interested in being an online

English teacher. I jumped at the chance. This was something new and exciting! I'd taught before, but never like this. My former client sent me to Take Lessons, where I ended up working part-time, on and off, for more than three years.

I began teaching English, one-on-one, mostly to students with learning differences, but also, just to students who needed some additional support. I started at $10 an hour, and within one year, I was making $45 an hour. I didn't work every day, and I never had more than one student a day, but there was such a demand, I could have had this full-time if I wanted it. Do you teach? Check out Take Lessons. IT's a way to freelance as a teacher.

Unfortunately, in 2013, I was roped into a wacky publishing deal, where I was promised the world (this is where I should have listened to my agent pal and let her read the contract), and I knew that I couldn't teach and edit my novel on a sharp deadline at the same time. So, I gave up Take Lessons for the novel. Fortunately for me, the novel was fun to write, even though the publisher folded, and I go back to TakeLessons.com every now and then when I feel like teaching again. Had I not followed up with my past client, I would never have discovered this wonderful opportunity. My resume' is richer now, my bills got paid, and I was able to indulge in another one of my passions—helping others find their writer voice.

⇒ **So, FOLLOW UP whenever you can! You never know where this professional kindness might lead you.**

Wrap Up

- **Follow up with past clients.**

- **They might have more work, or better yet, bigger leads for you.**

CHAPTER TEN

Don't Be Cheap

"Sincerity: Willingness to spend one's own money."

Mason Cooley

⇒ **Don't Go With Any Free Services.**

⇒**You get what you pay for, and if you don't pay for a membership with Guru or Up Work, you won't be allowed to get most clients.**

You won't be able to send out the amount of proposals you need to really make a living, and remember, you have to send out a lot of proposals every time you're looking for a new batch of jobs. Every. Time.

Online freelance services make their money by finding work for you and help for their clients. If you don't want to pay them for this effort, they aren't going to make the most lucrative jobs available to you. In fact, they aren't going to make hardly any jobs available to you.

⇒ **Upwork, for example, only costs $10 a month for a basic, individual, account. This allows you an infinite amount of possibilities with your profile, your portfolio, messaging between clients, and it allows you to be made available to be a featured freelancer once you start obtaining all those four and five star reviews.**

And it's absolutely not hard at all to obtain said reviews. You just have to do good and consistent work. If you're kind, your client will be kind. You'll review them and they'll review you, and you'll get those ratings. However, if you only sign up for the free account, you'll never get there. And before we go any further (because we are going to go further with this), you should know that I only mention Upwork so much, because it's the service I most prefer. As I have said before, I have a pretty severe disability, a neuromuscular disease called Myasthenia Gravis. It's a day-by-day, minute-by-minute, disease. Sometimes, my muscles just stop working and I have to take a break from freelancing for a time. Upwork allows me to do that with ease. The control is all mine, which is probably one of the main reasons I love freelancing so much. Other services are not as flexible, and it's this flexibility and ease of use, that makes me really appreciate their service so much. So, no. I'm not on the payroll or anything. I just really like Upwork that much. I loved them when they were Elance and I love them even more now that they're Upwork. Also, your monthly fee is just that, monthly. You can cancel next month. You can pick up again in three months. Whatever works for you. There's no loss in getting a paid account.

Now that we've got that out of the way...Pay for your account. It's not much. It's monthly, and sometimes these services run specials where they'll give you a month free, or extra "connect points" (points that allow you to connect to new clients) if you refer a friend. After you send out proposals to various jobs, you'll get a prompt to share what you're working on with your Facebook or Twitter pals. You'll get freebies, and such, if you encourage others to sign up. I've never done this, because I like to keep my work pretty private, but others I know have done it and it's really yielded some nice extras for them. So, pay for your account. Good business is rarely free.

And don't be cheap with yourself. Buy the tools you need and the supplies you need to do your job well. Make space for your work, get the pencils, pens, and notebooks you need. For God's sake, don't forget the coffee or tea! Make time to exercise and eat. Reward yourself for hard work.

You don't have to break the bank, but you do have to treat yourself with the respect you deserve. Start with the right account for you, and get yourself the tools you need to succeed without going bankrupt. Use wisdom. This includes getting an accountant or using a service like TurboTax when you go to file your taxes in January. Save every receipt for anything related to money you spent on your business/freelancing career. You'll be asked to complete a W-9 when you first sign up with any of these services as well. Request that it be sent to you in early January, so that you have proof of income for your accountant, or accounting service, like H&R Block or wherever. Also, you can add this proof of income to your credit report if you're self-employed. Simply go to Credit Karma, or another place like that, and follow the instructions for adding pertinent information to your report.

Wrap Up

- **Pay for your account.**

- **Free accounts will yield you absolutely nothing.**

- **You can cancel anytime.**

- **It's not a yearly membership with Upwork and others. It's only monthly.**

CHAPTER ELEVEN

Relax. It's a Job, Not a Marriage or Your Soul Salvation

"To have faith is to trust yourself to the water.
When you swim you don't grab hold of the water,
because if you do you will sink and drown.
Instead you relax and float."

Alan Watts

⇒ **Enjoy: Remember that list you made of all the things you were willing to do and the things you weren't?**

Well make an additional list of the things you want out of life. Be specific with why you want to freelance in the first place. Put that specific on a sticky note and keep it on, or near, your workspace. Remind yourself daily why you're doing this. If you're like most people, you're doing it to find a work-life-balance and to live out your writing dream. Don't forget that. Don't lose focus and become a workaholic. Yes, you have to be persistent and dedicated.

⇒ **You have to be focused and ambitious, but you don't have to become the worst parent or boyfriend of the year just because your client needs you.**

Keep a priority list. Make it in the shape of a pyramid and remember the most important thing(s) in your life. Don't trade them in for money or work.

I'm not going to tell you that you can have everything just because you visualized it. That works in a lot of cases, I believe, but life throws a lot of curve balls. If you're alive, you know this to be true. Faith, flexibility, and kindness will help you weather the storms exponentially. Be faithful to yourself and others. Be flexible, because the freelancing life requires it. Be kind, because no one likes a jerk. You don't and your client doesn't.

If you've lived a day on this earth, you know this is all true. You can live the life you want if you work hard, produce quality work, remain persistent, and stay positive. Freelancing is not the life for Debbie Downers, people who feel sorry for themselves, or lazy bums. It's a job for people--introverts and extroverts--who are willing to think for themselves, assess their skills adequately, articulate them to potential clients, learn from mistakes, and rejoice in their own achievements when they come.

Wrap Up

- **Work hard but don't neglect the people you love for a job or jobs.**

- **Jobs are replaceable, people aren't.**

"Start by doing what's necessary; then do what's possible, and suddenly you are doing the impossible."

St. Francis of Assisi

Conclusion

I wish you all the success in your freelancing career. Millions of people embark on this kind of lifestyle every year. You can do it, too, and you can do it well. My tips will work for you, if you believe in yourself and in your abilities. You can start small and grow your business. Take a year and climb the ladder slowly, if you like. Take on one $10 job a week for two months. Get a handful of four and five star reviews and clients who are ecstatic with your work. Take on jobs that pay $40 an article for another two months.

If you're even able to work this slowly and build your career this slowly, I'll be surprised, because once you get the freelancing bug, you just can't drop it. Those first few outstanding reviews will bring you much confidence and a boatload of courage. This will turn into success, if you remain professional.

Believe in you and others will too. God Bless You!

Some resources for you:

- **National Writers Union**

  https://nwu.org/

- **Freelancer's Union**

  https://www.freelancersunion.org/

- **Local Writer's Group** --- **Google your county, or city, and "writer's groups". Visit a few. Find one that works for you. If you can't find one, start one. Advertise on Facebook and meet up at a local coffeehouse or even meet up through Skype or online.**

- **Writer's Digest**

  http://www.writersdigest.com/

- **Upwork**

  www.upwork.com

- **Guru**

  www.guru.com

- **Fiverr**

  www.fiverr.com

Sample Proposal

I would love to take on this project for you! I am an expert in X, Y, Z (whatever expertise your client is asking for and you must ACTUALLY have it!), and I've created countless websites, blog posts, articles, etc....focusing on X,Y,Z. I'm a highly rated writer, efficient in every aspect, and work well on hard deadlines. I can complete this job for you in X Amount of Time.

I hold a BA in Blah-Blah and a Masters in Bee-Bee. I've written for more than 10 magazines and newspapers (or whatever you've written for—paid or unpaid), and I have two published, award-winning (if they are) novels. Below, you can find links to my blog, website, and other places where I've been published.

I would be happy to write a brief 200 word sample article for you, and I've attached several of my best portfolio pieces to this proposal. Thank you so much for taking the time to review my offer. I look forward to working with you.

Have a wonderful day,

Ms. Wordsmith

References:

Warmingham, Colleen. Minimologist.

http://www.minimologist.com/.

www.BrainyQuote.com

Franz, Thaeda, PhD. "Facebook Interview." Interview by Tiffani Velez. May 26, 2016.

ABOUT THE AUTHOR

Tiffani Velez has been a successful freelance writer since 1996. Her nonfiction work has appeared in *Pennsylvania Magazine, Country Discoveries, Yahoo! News, St. Anthony Messenger* and many other online and print magazines in the United States, Canada, and Europe. She's the author of three novels, *Budapest, A Berlin Story,* and *All This Time.* She's currently completing her MFA in Writing from Lindenwood University.

www.ingramcontent.com/pod-product-compliance
Lightning Source LLC
Chambersburg PA
CBHW071114280526
45787CB00003B/1030